THE PANORAMA

OF THE CITY OF **NEW YORK**

EDITED BY
LYNN MALISZEWSKI
WITH LAUREN HAYNES

WITH TEXT BY
MARC H. MILLER
KENNETH T. JACKSON
VALERIE PALEY
AND VYJAYANTHI RAO

Queens Museum
New York

Scala Arts Publishers, Inc.
New York

CONTENTS

FOREWORD

This book marks the sixtieth anniversary of the 1964–1965 New York World's Fair in Flushing Meadows Corona Park, which included the debut of *The Panorama of the City of New York*. The model itself is an anomaly as far as historical objects are concerned: as viewers we are awestruck by its scale, which situates one outside of time and space, yet it remains familiar. If we compare the model we see—depicting January 1, 1992—and our contemporary city, we can note many absences: the developments in Queens, specifically Long Island City and Flushing; the new archi-

tectural additions in Manhattan including Hudson Yards and the High Line, and Atlantic Terminal and Cadman Plaza in Brooklyn. Even as films and television shows have made the New York City skyline somewhat ubiquitous, the *Panorama* proves there are always new perspectives to discover.

The *Panorama* has been used in many ways by various audiences. It remains an important teaching tool for schoolchildren across the boroughs in both second and fourth grade. Studying this artifact can illuminate how geography and natural resources

Spencer Lowell, *Untitled (023)*, 2016. Archival pigment print. © Spencer Lowell.

affect a population, how community is constructed alongside the built environment, and how people are connected by culture, history, and proximity. The *Panorama* inspires questions, and has been a subject matter and point of inquiry for artists for as long as the Queens Museum has existed. Housing justice, the economy, immigration, and empire-building have been subjected to deeper interrogation, with the *Panorama* serving as a site.

The *Panorama* has been maintained for sixty years, and there are many people who had a hand in making sure this incredible model remained intact for future generations. We'd like to thank the funders who have helped upgrade and preserve the *Panorama* since the Queens Museum took over stewardship of the model in 1972. Additionally, the hundreds of individual donors who have supported the ongoing care and maintenance of the *Panorama* through our Adopt-A-Building Program deserve our deepest thanks as well. The New York State Legislature, the New York City Department of Cultural Affairs, Queens Borough presidents past and present, and the New York City Council have also provided consistent support to the Museum and our efforts.

I want to express my deepest appreciation for the current and former staff of the Queens Museum who have helped to maintain this model. I'd like to thank the following QM staffers specifically—without them, the *Panorama* might not have survived. Janet Schneider, former director of QM (1977–89), kept a close eye on the *Panorama* and initiated the renovations we see today (the Crystal Walkway donated by Crystal Window & Door Systems with Rafael Viñoly, 1988–89, and full update of the model with Lester Associates, 1992–94). Beth M. Henriques, former assistant director of QM (1988–90), coordinated and managed the 1992 renovation alongside Lester Associates. Marc H. Miller, curator of the World's Fair Collection (1985–94), played a major role in the fundraising and curatorial vision prior to the *Panorama*'s 1992 renovation, and initiated the New York World's Fair Association in 1988 with its headquarters at QM. Phyllis Bilick, the official staff photographer at QM starting in 1984 through the *Panorama*'s 1992 renovation, captured a number of images shared in this volume.

More recently, we have to thank Debra Wimpfheimer, deputy director of QM, who has been a part of the partnerships and planning team since 2002, spearheading the Adopt-A-Building Program. We are grateful for Louise Weinberg, former curator and archives manager at QM (2008–19), who paid special attention to the *Panorama* during and after our most recent museum renovation. Lastly, we'd like to thank former QM directors Carma C. Fauntleroy, Tom Finkelpearl, and Laura Raicovich, who supported *Panorama*-focused publications and exploratory exhibitions including *City Speculations* (1996); *Designing the Future: The Queens Museum of Art and the New York City Building* (2002); *Michael Rakowitz: Romanticized all out of proportion* (2003); *Robert Moses and the Modern City: The Road to Recreation* (2007); *Stephen Talasnik, Panorama: The Mapping of Prediction* (2009); *Structure Has a Life with Personality: Art about architecture from the Queens Museum collection* (2010); *Wonderstruck in the Panorama: Drawings by Brian Selznick* (2011); *Bringing the World into the World* (2014); *Never Built New York* (2017); and *The Panorama Handbook: Thoughts and Visions on and around the Queens Museum's Panorama of the City of New York* (2018). We send our deepest thanks to all the artists and educators who have created artworks and developed tours and interpretation inspired by the *Panorama*.

We are grateful to the team for their work to make this publication possible. Thank you to our contributors: Marc H. Miller, Kenneth T. Jackson, Valerie Paley, and Vyjayanthi Rao. Additional thanks are due to our partners Scala Arts Publishers, Inc.—specifically Jennifer Norman, designers Rebecca Sylvers and Miko McGinty, and editors Beth Holmes and Erin Barnett—for their collaboration and enthusiasm. This volume would not have been possible without the dedication and hard work of coeditors Lynn Maliszewski and Lauren Haynes and the assistance and research of Mayisha Hassan. Thank you to the City of New York for their support of activities related to the *Panorama*. We are grateful to The Robert David Lion Gardiner Foundation for their support of this publication. We dedicate this book to the memory of Steven M. Polan, who loved visiting the *Panorama* over the decades and who so generously provided the necessary support for this publication.

Sally Tallant
President and executive director, Queens Museum

Previous

**Midtown West, Manhattan,
*The Panorama of the City of
New York*, 2015.**

Digital photograph. © Max Touhey.

Left

**Worker at Lester Associates pulls
a reference image from a set of
aerial photographs used for the
construction of *The Panorama of
the City of New York*, ca. 1963.**

Scanned medium-format negative.
Gift of Bernard Spence, Lester
Associates.

View of the Lester Associates workshop during the construction of *The Panorama of the City of New York*, ca. 1963.

Vintage silver gelatin print. Gift of Bernard Spence, Lester Associates.

Workers at their woodworking jigs in the Lester Associates workshop, ca. 1963.

Scanned large-format negative.
Gift of Lester Associates.

Workers at the Lester Associates
workshop transition buildings
from templates to the panels of
*The Panorama of the City of New
York,* ca. 1963.

Scanned 35mm negative. Gift of
Lester Associates.

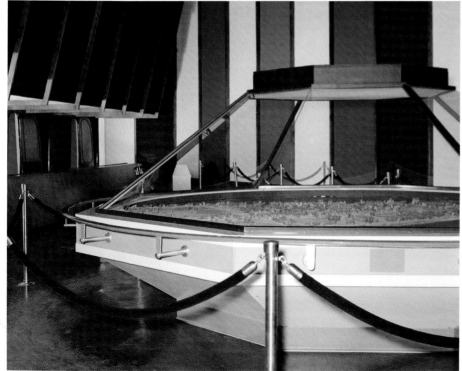

Above
Panel fabrication for *The Panorama of the City of New York* at the Lester Associates workshop, ca. 1962.

Scanned 35mm negative. Gift of Lester Associates.

Left
Entryway to *The Panorama of the City of New York* with the Castello Plan model in the foreground, ca. 1964.

Vintage silver gelatin print.

PANORAMA ORIGIN STORY

The *Panorama* was built as New York City's display at the 1964-1965 World's Fair. After the Fair it served as an urban planning tool.

Approximately 14,000 people visited the model daily during the Fair.

The model was conceived of by Robert Moses and constructed by Lester Associates of West Nyack, NY. It was paid for by New York City's Board of Estimate.

Dates of construction:
July 1961-April 1964

The *Panorama* was designed to stay current with the changing city. Complete updates took place in 1967, 1968, 1969, 1974, and 1992.

MODEL AS OBJECT

It took over one hundred full-time workers to construct the _Panorama_.

Scale:
1 inch = 100 feet (1:1200)

Total area:
9,335 square feet

Section pieces:
Originally 273, but only 272 installed due to the size of the room

Estimated weight:
45,000 lbs.

Cost:
$672,662.69 in 1964 US dollars

Model-makers prepare a section of *The Panorama of the City of New York* in the Lester Associates workshop, ca. 1963.

Scanned large-format negative. Gift of Lester Associates.

Aerial view, *The Panorama of the City of New York*, April 25, 1964.
Vintage silver gelatin print. © Ben Cohen. Gift of the New York City Parks Archive.

Construction of the gallery to house *The Panorama of the City of New York*, ca. 1962.

Scanned medium-format negative. Gift of Lester Associates.

Above

Architectural rendering, second floor viewing of *The Panorama of the City of New York*, ca. 1962.

Watercolor on paper. © M. M. Gift of Lester Associates.

Right

Preliminary model of *The Panorama of the City of New York*, ca. 1961.

Vintage silver gelatin print. Gift of Lester Associates.

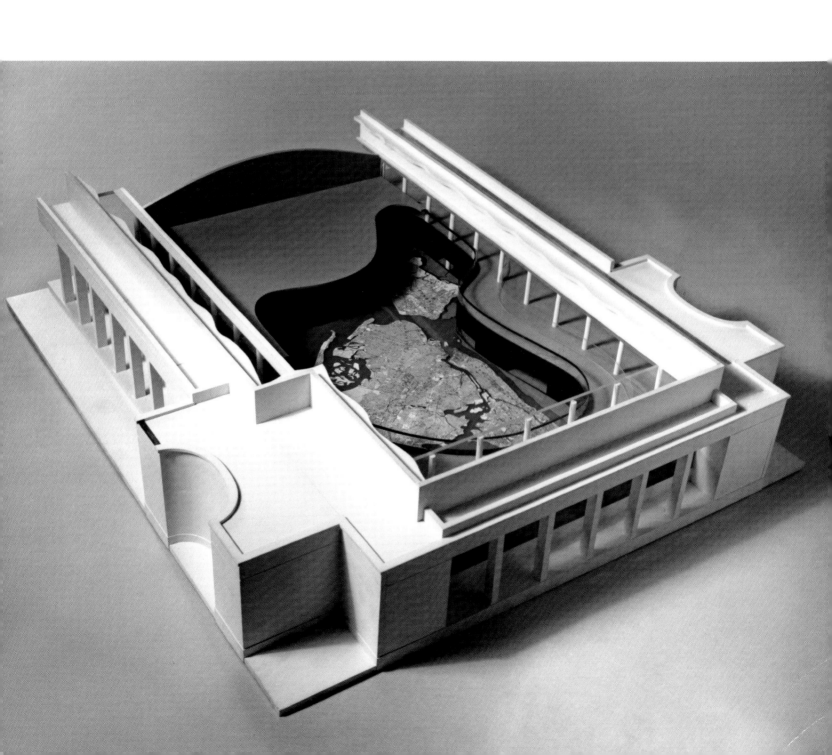

Worker places models of buildings on a section of *The Panorama of the City of New York* in the Lester Associates workshop, ca. 1963.

Scanned medium-format negative. Gift of Bernard Spence, Lester Associates.

31

Brooklyn, *The Panorama of the City of New York,* **1994.**

Scanned large-format color positive film. © Andrea Brizzi.

Left

Workers at Lester Associates cross-check municipal maps alongside details of *The Panorama of the City of New York*, ca. 1963.

Scanned large-format negative. Gift of Lester Associates.

Below

Architectural rendering of *The Panorama of the City of New York* within the New York City Pavilion, ca. 1962.

Scanned large-format negative. Gift of Lester Associates.

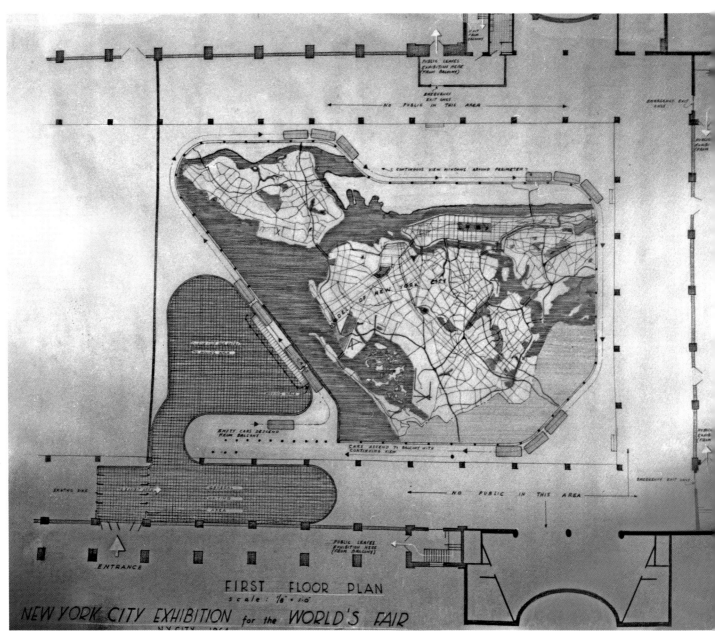

FIRST FLOOR PLAN
scale: ⅛" = 1'0"

NEW YORK CITY EXHIBITION for the WORLD'S FAIR

Worker places model buildings on a section of *The Panorama of the City of New York*, ca. 1963.

Scanned 35mm negative. Gift of Lester Associates.

Measuring the height of the Empire State Building on *The Panorama of the City of New York*, ca. 1970.

Scanned large-format negative. Gift of Lester Associates.

Left

Worker stands over John F. Kennedy International Airport in the Lester Associates workshop, ca. 1963.

Scanned large-format negative. Gift of Lester Associates.

Top

Laying out streets on a section of *The Panorama of the City of New York*, ca. 1963.

Vintage silver gelatin print. Gift of Lester Associates.

Bottom

Two workers consult aerial photographs of New York City for a section of *The Panorama of the City of New York*, ca. 1963.

Scanned 35mm slide. Gift of Lester Associates.

Preliminary work on John F. Kennedy International Airport, *The Panorama of the City of New York*, ca. 1962.

Scanned large-format negative. Gift of Lester Associates.

John F. Kennedy International Airport, *The Panorama of the City of New York,* **ca. 1980s.**

Vintage silver gelatin print.

John F. Kennedy International Airport on *The Panorama of the City of New York* **with preparatory maps during the 1992–94 restoration, ca. 1992.**

Vintage silver gelatin print.
© Phyllis Bilick.

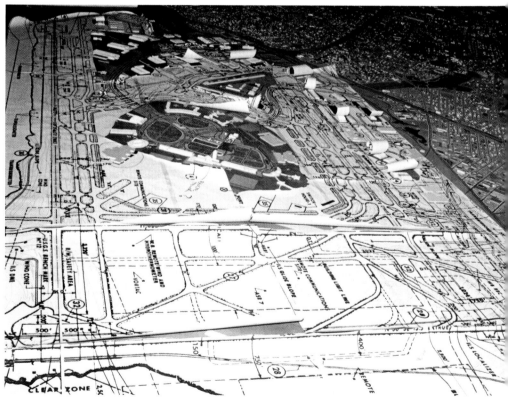

Above

Jamaica Bay, west of Cross Bay Boulevard, looking west toward Brooklyn and Manhattan on _The Panorama of the City of New York_, September 1989.

Scanned 35mm negative.
© Phyllis Bilick.

Left

Worker details LaGuardia Airport on _The Panorama of the City of New York_, ca. 1963.

Vintage silver gelatin print. Gift of Lester Associates.

SPECIAL FEATURES

Moving airplanes land every minute at LaGuardia Airport in Queens.

Two workers at Lester Associates left their names spelled in shrubbery—"Bill" and "Ed"—on two islands in Jamaica Bay.

Originally, at the World's Fair, visitors would view the *Panorama* from a "helicopter" ride that moved around the perimeter of the model.

Inside each four-person fiberglass cabin, attendees would hear "The City of Opportunity," a nine-minute monologue voiced by broadcasting legend Lowell Thomas.

The model was meant to be walked on, permitting close-up views of any area by a person or group of people.

UPDATING THE *PANORAMA* AFTER THE WORLD'S FAIR

In order to construct and install new buildings onto the *Panorama,* Lester Associates offered three examples (in 1964 US Dollars):

$40: a housing development of forty two-story, attached brick homes

$80: a housing project of eight buildings, each fourteen stories high

$120: a major office building comparable to Chase Manhattan bank, sixty stories (including rework to adjacent buildings)

The Bronx, looking southeast toward Queens, with the Robert F. Kennedy Bridge (formerly the Triborough Bridge) and Bronx-Whitestone Bridge connecting the two boroughs, *The Panorama of the City of New York*, 2016.

Digital photograph. © Max Touhey.

Previous
Cross section of *The Panorama of the City of New York*, 1961.
Watercolor on paper. © M. M. Gift of Lester Associates.

Above
Entrance to the "helicopter" ride, *The Panorama of the City of New York*, in the lobby of the New York City Building, ca. 1964.
Vintage silver gelatin print. Gift of Lester Associates.

A view of the "helicopter" ride inside *The Panorama of the City of New York*, ca. 1988.

Scanned 35mm slide.
© Phyllis Bilick.

Worker applies masking tape guides of the Belt Parkway in Brooklyn near Floyd Bennett Field to a panel of *The Panorama of the City of New York* before painting roadways, ca. 1963.

Scanned large-format negative. Gift of Bernard Spence, Lester Associates.

Right
Detail, George Washington Bridge and Manhattan, *The Panorama of the City of New York,* **2015.**
Digital photograph. © Max Touhey.

Overleaf

Top Left **Flushing Meadows Corona Park, Queens,** *The Panorama of the City of New York,* **ca. 1980s.**
Scanned 35mm slide.

Bottom Left **The Long Island Rail Road (LIRR) Sunnyside Yard, Long Island City, Queens,** *The Panorama of the City of New York,* **ca. 1980s.**
Scanned 35mm slide.
Anonymous gift.

Right **View of the East River with Manhattan at left and Brooklyn at right,** *The Panorama of the City of New York,* **2016. Bridges from foreground to background: Brooklyn, Manhattan, Williamsburg.**
Digital photograph. © Max Touhey.

THE PANORAMA OF THE CITY OF NEW YORK

MARC H. MILLER

At the heart of the Queens Museum in Flushing Meadows Corona Park sits *The Panorama of the City of New York*, a three-dimensional scale model of the metropolis that was constructed for the New York City Building at the 1964–1965 World's Fair. Dubbed the "World's Largest Scale Model," the *Panorama* encompasses 9,335 square feet, occupying the former site of a roller-skating rink. At a scale of 1 inch to 100 feet, it reproduces the largest city in North America. The model includes all 320 square miles of New York City's five boroughs—the Bronx, Brooklyn, Manhattan, Queens, and Staten Island. It accurately duplicates the 771 miles of city shoreline, all of the streets, thousands of parks, hundreds of major bridges, and each of its approximately 830,000 individual buildings. The *Panorama* even includes miniature cars, boats, and a moving airplane landing every minute at LaGuardia Airport.

The *Panorama* was clearly a good investment for the city: it was not only one of the most successful exhibits at the World's Fair, but later served as a planning tool for the city. Since 1972, it has been a popular and useful attraction at the Queens Museum. The *Panorama* is admired as a masterpiece in a long tradition of model-making, and functions as a learning tool helping everyone—from tourists and schoolchildren to sophisticated urban planners—understand a complex city.

It is appropriate that the person behind the construction of the *Panorama* was Robert Moses (1888–1981), the man perhaps most responsible for shaping the physical structure of twentieth-century New York City. Starting in the early 1920s with the seaside recreational area at Jones Beach on Long Island, until his forced retirement over fifty years later, Moses—working in a variety of city and state positions—completely transformed the city through an ambitious building program of parks, roadways, bridges, public housing, and major civic structures. The achievements of Moses's half-century career are astounding: Orchard Beach, Flushing Meadows Corona Park, the Central Park Zoo, the Astoria Pool, the Grand Central Parkway, the Belt Parkway, the Long Island Expressway, the Triborough Bridge, the Verrazzano-Narrows Bridge, Stuyvesant Town, Co-op City, Lincoln Center, the United Nations complex, and Shea Stadium are only some. In his construction of public works, Moses used architectural models as aids in both the planning and promotion of projects. As his building projects grew in scale and ambition in the 1950s, the models he commissioned became more elaborate; it was during this phase of his career that he first employed the model-making firm Lester Associates.

Born in 1911, Raymond Lester made his first model at twelve, and landed his first professional model-making job with the Architectural and Scientific Corporation doing work for the 1939–1940 New York World's Fair. During the years of World War II, Lester worked for the naval architects Gibbs & Cox, making ship models for structural tests of the destroyers the company manufactured. Lester opened his own model shop in New York's Greenwich Village in 1945. Within a few years he built a much larger shop in Westchester County, New York, to serve a list of clients that had grown to include major architectural firms such as Harrison & Abramovitz, the United States government, IBM, and General Electric. Lester Associates made a full range of models—architectural, terrain, and engineering models, product prototypes and full-size operational test models as well as room-sized industrial control boards and industrial displays. In 1954, Lester did his first work for the Triborough Bridge & Tunnel Authority (TBTA). Over the next fifteen years, Lester served as Moses's principal model-maker, working for the variety of agencies headed by the building czar on a host of different projects, from small individual models to large public displays. The bulk of Lester's work was large terrain models of the ambitious highway and bridge projects of Moses's later years, including the Verrazzano-Narrows Bridge and the unbuilt Lower Manhattan and Mid-Manhattan Expressways.

Soon after his appointment as president of the 1964–1965 New York World's Fair Corporation in February of 1960, Moses started putting together the team needed to create the *Panorama*. The Board of Estimate allocated $2,278,366 to architect Daniel Chait to refurbish the New York City Building (built for the 1939–1940 New York World's Fair), and $620,000 to Lester Associates to construct the *Panorama* and the pavilion's other interior exhibits. The *Panorama* alone ultimately took over three years to complete, and cost $672,662.69. The displays were also conceived by Moses, although Parks Commissioner Newbold Morris was technically in charge of the pavilion.

As host of the Fair, New York City was determined to have a lavish display. Moses had served as Mayor Fiorello La Guardia's representative in the city's dealings with the 1939–1940 New York World's Fair Corporation, witnessing firsthand the popular success of the 1939 Fair's large model exhibits. Although the *Panorama* is a unique object linked to the culmination of Moses's career, it also fits comfortably into a tradition of World's Fair model-making. The most popular feature at the 1939 Fair was *Futurama*, a 35,000-square-foot model that Norman Bel Geddes designed for the General Motors Pavilion. Projecting twenty years into the future, the model illustrated how America would look in 1960. *The City of Light*, a huge diorama designed by Walter Dorwin Teague for the Consolidated Edison Pavilion, also presaged the *Panorama*. Built by the Diorama Corporation of America, *The City of Light* was a block-long contraction of New York with over four thousand recognizable buildings from Brooklyn to Westchester. While the foreground buildings were done fully in the round,

Midtown Manhattan, *The Panorama of the City of New York*, including a temporary plastic placeholder for Robert Moses's proposed Mid-Manhattan Expressway, ca. 1966. Vintage silver gelatin print. Gift of Lester Associates.

low relief was used for the background structures in front of the painted backdrop. The tallest building, the Empire State Building, measured twenty-nine feet tall. It featured a moving version of the electrically powered subway and elaborate lighting effects, which, like the *Panorama*, included a day-to-night cycle.

The *Panorama* clearly reflected the distinctive tastes of Robert Moses, which were also evident in a triumvirate of objects at the Fair, each of which, in its own way, was the world's largest example of a particular mode of cartography. Standing next to the New York City Pavilion is the Unisphere, a 140-foot-high, 990,000-pound steel representation of Earth, conceived by a long-time Moses associate Gilmore Clarke, and constructed by the US Steel Corporation. The Unisphere was the icon of the Fair and the "World's Largest Global Structure." At the nearby New York State Pavilion, Governor Nelson Rockefeller, architect Philip Johnson, and the Texaco Oil Corporation arranged for a giant floor mosaic

Architectural rendering, lobby of the New York City Pavilion and entrance to the "helicopter" ride around *The Panorama of the City of New York*, **1961. Watercolor on paper. Gift of Lester Associates.**

New York City Pavilion, New York World's Fair advertisement, ca. 1964. Poster.

illustrating the New York State road map distributed at Texaco gas stations. Larger than half a football field, the mosaic was the "World's Largest Road Map."

The 1964–1965 New York World's Fair celebrated the three hundredth anniversary of the British conquest of the Dutch city of New Amsterdam and the renaming of the city. The displays at the New York City Pavilion were designed to show the progress of three centuries. Upon entering the lobby, visitors were greeted by New York City Mayor Robert F. Wagner's audio, directing them to a model showing New Amsterdam in 1660. Borrowed from the Museum of the City of New York, the model, made in 1931 by Charles S. Capehart, was refurbished and elaborately encased by Lester Associates. Visitors then moved on to the *Panorama*, built at a much smaller scale than the model of New Amsterdam (1:1200 as opposed to 1:300) but dramatically larger. The contrast in size graphically demonstrated the city's growth from a trading post on the tip of Manhattan to a sprawling five-borough metropolis. For ten cents visitors could take an eight-minute tracked-car ride around the 500-foot perimeter of the giant model. Billed as a "helicopter trip" around the city, the ride simulated views from 3,000 to 20,000 feet. Riders heard "The City of Opportunity," a text read by news commentator Lowell Thomas. The *Panorama* was one of the Fair's most successful attractions. Fifty-four continuously running four-seater cars were designed to carry 1,400 people an hour, and there was often a 90-minute wait.

Visitors exited the *Panorama* onto the second floor of the New York City Building, where a corridor decorated to look like Times Square at night led them to the glass-enclosed balcony area overlooking the *Panorama*. Here they could watch the model go through its day-to-night lighting cycle, and listen to another Lowell Thomas audiotape celebrating the thriving city. Thomas's monologue explained that the tiny colored lights shining on the *Panorama* showed the 3,172 municipal facilities for such basic services as education, protection, recreation, and healthcare.

When viewers tired of the *Panorama*, they could see other displays in the New York City Pavilion built by Lester Associates. In a large room adjacent to the balcony overlook, a "Museum

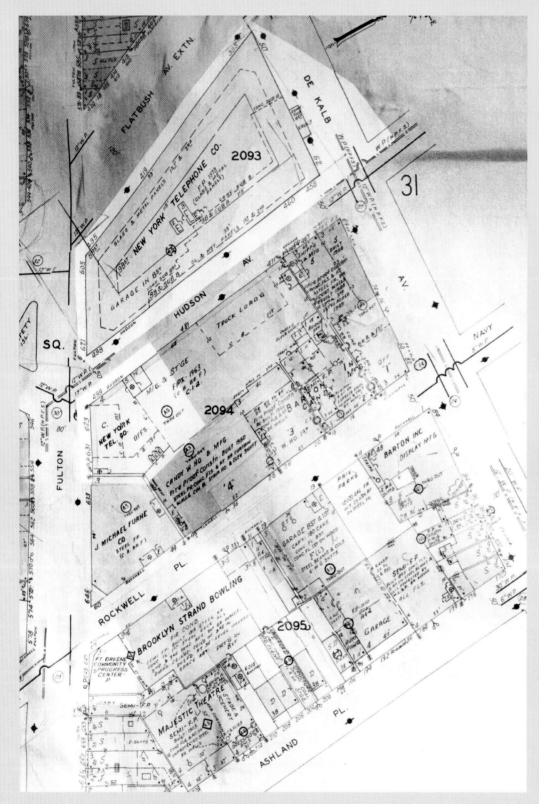

Detail, Insurance Map of the Borough of Brooklyn (Volume 2, Map no. 26), Sanborn Map Company, ca. 1987. Vintage silver gelatin print. © Phyllis Bilick.

Showcase" offered a sampling of objects from the city's different museums, historical societies, and libraries. An elaborate exhibit of models and animated display panels near the ground floor exit celebrated the past achievements of Moses, the TBTA, and his plans for the future of New York City.

Lester's contract with the city stipulated that the *Panorama* would later serve as an aid for urban planning. The *Panorama* was expected to accurately duplicate the topography of the New York City landscape, as well as the exact placement and appearance of all man-made structures. The contract allowed for a 1 percent margin of error.

Lester Associates gathered and processed all the information needed for the *Panorama*; constructed the vast, complex model; and ultimately assembled it in the New York City Building. Specialized city maps designed for tax and insurance purposes showed the city block-by-block, and included the ground plan of every structure, its height, and the materials used. These maps laid the groundwork for the *Panorama*. To verify the city maps and understand the distribution of trees and foliage, 109 vertical aerial photographs of New York City were purchased from the Aero Service Corporation of Philadelphia, Pennsylvania. To portray the building elevations accurately, 5,000 oblique aerial photographs (shot at an angle) were commissioned from Aero Service, and pictures of individual structures were gathered from libraries and public agencies. Nineteen contour maps produced by the US Geological Survey were used to record topography. A set of thirty-five maps from Sanborn Map Company was used to determine the location of municipal services.

The surface of the *Panorama* was constructed at Lester's Westchester workshop in 273 separate sections. The 186 central sections each measure 4 × 10 feet, while the edges are unique and cut according to the city's borders. The sections are made of Formica flakeboard topped by urethane foam slabs—a newly introduced, malleable material that was easy to cut and paint. The modelmakers' first task was to duplicate topography using the geological survey maps as a source. Shorelines and contour elevations were traced onto the surface, and the urethane foam was then routed and sanded.

The next stage of the process involved tracing the city's streets, highways, sidewalks, blocks, and parks onto the *Panorama* sections using G. W. Bromley and the Sanborn Map Company maps. Most of these map books used the same 1-inch-to-100-foot scale as the *Panorama*. Sometimes, though, scale varied, and photostated copies were needed before paper templates could be made for basic tracing. The model was painted according to a strict color code that designated types of roads and buildings.

Next came the task of forming and gluing down over 800,000 miniature buildings. The vast majority of the city's structures were represented with standardized model units that Lester carefully designed and then molded out of plastic. Most of the buildings on the *Panorama* are one- and two-story homes and small industrial buildings, which were depicted from an assortment of

Standardized building shapes for
The Panorama of the City of New York
in the Lester Associates workshop,
ca. 1963. Scanned 35mm slide. Gift of
Lester Associates.

150 differently shaped and sized units. Brownstones, tenements, and four- or five-floor apartments were represented with another forty different unit styles. Other standardized units were created for single-steepled churches, double-steepled churches, and an assortment of water tower designs. There are 100,000 large, basically geometric buildings that were handmade by combining 24 standardized shapes in varying ways. Finally 25,000 iconic New York City buildings—skyscrapers, large factories, colleges, hospitals, museums, major churches, and other notable landmarks—were custom-made. At this scale, however, there isn't much room for detail. The Empire State Building, the largest building in New York at the time the *Panorama* was constructed, measures approximately fifteen inches. Lester made no attempt to accurately portray windows, relying instead on standardized stencils.

By far the most accurate and finely made structures on the *Panorama* are its thirty-five bridges. While most of the *Panorama*'s buildings are made of wood and plastic, the bridges are constructed out of brass and shaped by a unique chemical milling process. Using the original blueprints of the bridges, Lester made detailed line drawings of their different sections and then reverse-exposed these drawings onto sheets of metal that were dipped in chemicals to dissolve the unexposed areas. Once the sections were assembled, the bridge models accurately reproduced the metal structure and cables of the originals.

One difficult facet of the construction of the *Panorama* involved the identification of city buildings by colored lights. Using facilities lists gathered from the major city departments as well as a set of Sanborn's city facility maps, Lester identified 3,172 city-owned structures. Tiny light bulbs were placed beneath the *Panorama* (where they could easily be changed), and a primitive form of fiber optics sent the glow of these lights to the surface of the model along translucent colored plastic wire inserted in the appropriate spots. Different colors identified the services provided by each city facility, but the number of services far exceeded the available colors. Five distinct light cycles were created, each related to a different group of services.

Overhead, the lights were designed to run in a cycle which simulates a dawn-to-dusk effect. The nighttime effect is enhanced by black lights illuminating ultraviolet paints on the city's parks. All the windows of the larger buildings are stenciled with a phosphorescent paint that glows in the dark. In 1964, this was a modern, effective, and relatively easy way to reproduce the city lights at night.

Each section of the *Panorama* was supported by adjustable metal legs and bolted to the adjoining ones. The touch-up process involved taping, puttying, and painting to seal the joints between each of the sections. Except for one hitch, the installation went smoothly: the space allotted for the model and amusement ride

Left
Raymond Lester holding the George Washington Bridge included on *The Panorama of the City of New York*, ca. 1964. Scanned 35mm slide. Gift of Lester Associates.

Right
Ink drawings used to construct bridges on *The Panorama of the City of New York*, ca. 1987. Top to bottom: Williamsburg Bridge, Brooklyn Bridge, Bayonne Bridge, Williamsburg Bridge, Manhattan Bridge, Triborough Bridge Approach Way. Vintage silver gelatin print. © Phyllis Bilick.

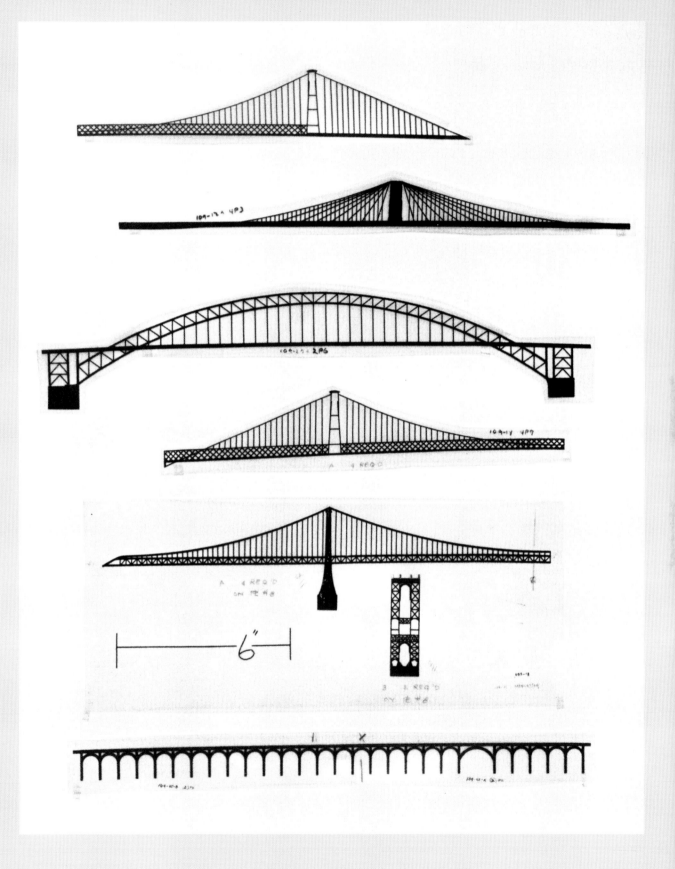

Nighttime cycle, *The Panorama of the City of New York*, October 25, 2017. Digital photograph. © Gary Gershoff/Getty Images for Amazon Studios (on the occasion of *Wonderstruck*, filmed at Queens Museum).

Installation view, *The Making of the Panorama of the City of New York: An Exhibition Documenting the History of the World's Largest Scale Model* (Queens Museum: March 19–October 2, 1988), ca. 1988. Dr. Marc H. Miller, curator of the exhibition, and Donna Tuman, former curator of education, examine the never-installed Far Rockaway section of the *Panorama*. Scanned 35mm slide. © Phyllis Bilick.

was a bit too small. This meant that one of the 273 sections—showing a part of Far Rockaway—was never installed.

The July 1961 construction contract for the *Panorama* stated, "the complete model shall be designed as a comprehensive planning and study device for use after the closing of the World's Fair." It was built so it could be easily dismantled and displayed elsewhere, but remained at the New York City Building where it was periodically used by Moses and others for regional planning. When Flushing Meadow reopened as a public park in 1967, the model and its "helicopter" ride were opened to the public. Although the *Panorama* was technically under the auspices of the New York City Planning Commission, the TBTA paid for its maintenance. In 1972, the Queens Museum was founded in the New York City Building and the model came under its supervision.

Inherent in its conception as a planning tool and educational device was the intent to keep the *Panorama* current with the city's constant changes. Despite being built in the early 1960s, Moses and Lester projected ahead so the model would be up-to-date when the Fair opened. Thus, the Van Wyck Expressway extension and the Verrazzano-Narrows Bridge, both still under construction, as well as future highways proposed for Staten Island, appear as finished structures. Lester designed the model so that buildings could be easily removed and roads reworked without excessive cost. Its vast, five-borough expanse is most useful for the type of broad regional planning that Moses specialized in.

Starting in the early 1920s, Moses had envisioned changes in the city to be brought about by the advent of the automobile, which had only recently replaced the horse and buggy. Moses believed the *Panorama* could be useful for determining the location of future housing, routes for highway construction, sightlines for television and radio transmission, traffic pattern studies, locating new firehouses and schools, and even for the police work of plotting motorcade routes and protecting overlooks. Moses, however, used the model infrequently. His creation became a celebration and commemoration of his past achievements; in every section of the *Panorama*, Moses's ambitious projects are emphasized. The bridges, seven of which Moses had constructed, are the only elements of the *Panorama* fabricated in metal. Parks, another of Moses's interests, are painted in an ultraviolet green so they glow during the night cycle.

Between 1967 and 1969, Lester provided yearly updates, basing his changes primarily on information the Sanborn Map Company regularly provides to subscribers of its Land Books. In 1974, following the founding of the Queens Museum, Lester provided another update for the *Panorama*—this time paid for by the city, not the TBTA. Since the update in 1974, changes to the *Panorama* have been sporadic and entirely dependent on voluntary donations of models. During the late 1970s there were relatively few major changes in the city, but the 1980s embraced a burst of building activity on the everchanging shoreline of Manhattan, and the Downtown and Midtown skylines. Some major architectural icons, such as the Citicorp building in Queens, were donated to the Museum in the 1980s. For the twenty-fifth anniversary of the *Panorama* in 1989, over 125 models were donated by corporations, real estate developers, and architects including IBM, AT&T, Marriott Hotel, Emery Roth & Sons, Skidmore Owings & Merrill, Swanke Hayden & Connell, and Fox & Fowle. These custom-made models remained on the *Panorama* following the 1992–94 restorations and can be identified since they are much more detailed than the models created by Lester.

As an attraction at the Queens Museum, the *Panorama* continues to help viewers better understand the metropolis and define their relationship to it. The miniature city has a striking clarity that inherently leads to new insights and observations. *Panorama* visitors learn as they marvel at the complex city. The model is especially useful for children, and the New York City Board of Education has incorporated it into its curriculum. During the 1988/89 school year, over 26,000 elementary and high school students from all sections of New York visited the Museum to see the *Panorama*.[1] Most children know only limited sections of the city and their understanding of the whole is often disjointed since they usually travel from one part to another by subway. The model gives these children a better understanding of their environment, introducing them to the harbor of New York and the five boroughs of the city.

In 1989, the *Panorama* underwent a complete rehabilitation. Under a plan conceived by Rafael Viñoly Architects, viewer access was improved with the addition of an ascending ramp with glass platforms overlooking the model. The old "helicopter" ride, unavailable for public use since the early 1970s, has been removed, and a grid of spotlights overhead illuminate the model with new clarity. With funds from the city and the Office of the Queens Borough President, the *Panorama* was also cleaned and completely updated to reflect January 1, 1992. At the Queens Museum, the *Panorama* presents a special challenge—it is a living exhibit that reflects the dynamic presence of New York City itself.

This essay was originally published in 1990 by the Queens Museum prior to the most recent renovation (1992–94); statistics reflect this note. The author has included some minor additions to provide insight into how that most recent renovation altered the make-up of the model.

1. The 2022/23 school year (November 2022–May 2023) saw over 4,000 elementary school students attending the Queens Museum for official tours.

Janet Schneider, former executive director of the Queens Museum, and representatives from Gerald D. Hines Interests place a model of "53rd at Third" (also known as "the Lipstick Building") onto *The Panorama of the City of New York*, 1987. Scanned 35mm slide. © Phyllis Bilick. Gift of Lester Associates.

Looking south toward the
Financial District, Manhattan,
*The Panorama of the City of
New York*, 2016.
Digital photograph. © Max Touhey.

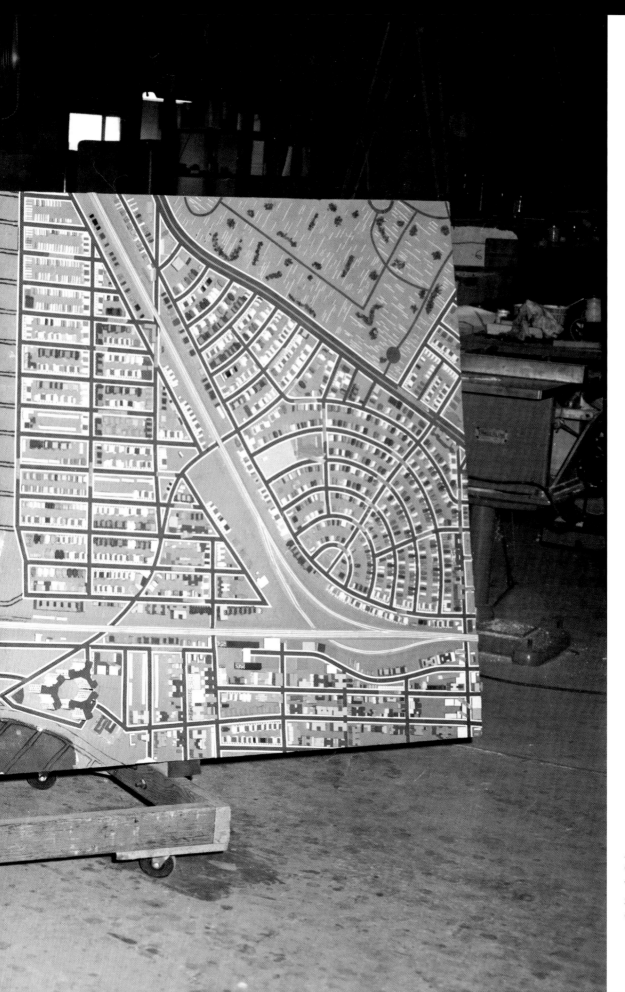

An unfinished panel of Rego Park, Queens, in the Lester Associates workshop, ca. 1963.

Scanned large-format negative. Gift of Lester Associates.

Above

Worker sands elevation contours on *The Panorama of the City of New York* in the Lester Associates workshop, ca. 1963.

Scanned large-format negative. Gift of Bernard Spence, Lester Associates.

Opposite

Worker sands elevation contours on *The Panorama of the City of New York* in the Lester Associates workshop, ca. 1963.

Vintage silver gelatin print. Gift of Lester Associates.

Queens, *The Panorama of the City of New York*, 2016.
Digital photograph. © Max Touhey.

**Model-makers prepare a section
of *The Panorama of the City of
New York* in the Lester Associates
workshop, ca. 1963.**

Scanned large-format negative.
Gift of Lester Associates.

Support: 497 steel legs

A steel plate sits on top of the metal legs. The bottom of each piece of the *Panorama* was originally poplar wood but transitioned to pine boards in the most recent renovation.

Formica flakeboard was placed upon the pine, then urethane foam. The foam was sculpted to mirror the topography of New York City.

All bodies of water originally had a textured surface that simulated waves.

All bridges are made of brass.

Cars, buses, trucks, railroad cars, and subway cars made of acrylic plastic were placed throughout the original model. They are still visible, albeit in smaller numbers than the first version of the *Panorama*.

When the *Panorama* debuted, boats, ships, barges, ferries, and tugs made out of cast metal were installed to depict a "typical New York Harbor scene."

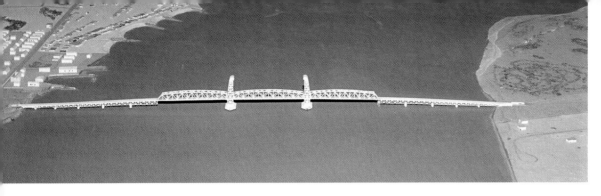

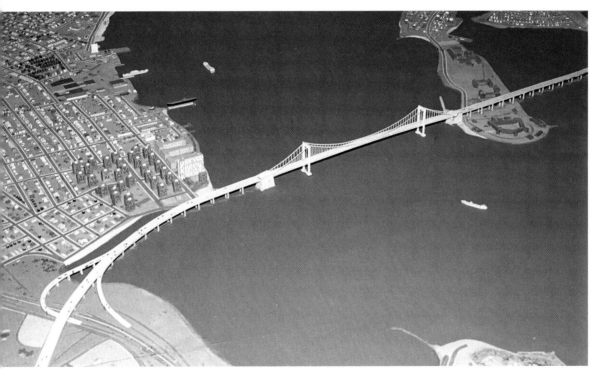

Hell Gate Bridge (front) and the Robert F. Kennedy Bridge (formerly the Triborough Bridge) (back), *The Panorama of the City of New York,* **September 1989.**

Scanned 35mm negative.
© Phyllis Bilick.

Midtown East, Manhattan,
The Panorama of the City of
New York, 2013.
Digital photograph. © Scott Rudd.

Worker at Lester Associates transfers buildings from a template to a panel of *The Panorama of the City of New York*, ca. 1963.

Vintage silver gelatin print. Gift of Lester Associates.

Left

Midtown Manhattan, including the Citigroup Center building (formerly Citicorp Center), *The Panorama of the City of New York,* **2016.**

Digital photograph. © Max Touhey.

Below

Placing the Citigroup Center building (formerly Citicorp Center) on *The Panorama of the City of New York,* **ca. 1977.**

Scanned 35mm slide.
Anonymous gift.

STRUCTURAL DETAILS: BUILDINGS ON THE *PANORAMA*

Approximate number of buildings:

1964: 830,000
1989: 865,000
2024: 895,000

Customized buildings that were donated to the Queens Museum in the 1970s and 1980s remain on the model. These buildings are mostly contained in Midtown and Downtown Manhattan.

Building breakdown:

Custom structures (skyscrapers, colleges, museums, churches, large factories): 25,000

Materials: a combination of wood, paper, and custom paint

Tenements, brownstones, and private homes: 620,000

Materials: acrylic plastic, produced by injection molds

Uniform structures (churches, hospitals, municipal offices): 150,000

Materials: cast epoxy

Unique buildings (museums, skyscrapers, cathedrals): 100,000

Materials: plexiglass

All numbers are approximate.

Detail, the Woolworth Building, Manhattan, *The Panorama of the City of New York,* **ca. 1980s.**

Scanned 35mm slide.

Detail, St. Patrick's Cathedral, Manhattan, *The Panorama of the City of New York,* **ca. 1980s.**

Scanned 35mm slide.

Mill Basin, Queens, *The Panorama of the City of New York,* **2016.**

Digital photograph. © Max Touhey.

Midtown Manhattan, including the Moynihan Train Hall (formerly the James A. Farley Post Office Building) and Madison Square Garden, *The Panorama of the City of New York*, 2016.

Digital photograph. © Max Touhey.

The Financial District, looking north across Manhattan, *The Panorama of the City of New York*, 1992.

Scanned large-format negative. © Phyllis Bilick.

THE PANORAMA OF THE CITY OF NEW YORK: LESSONS TO BE LEARNED FROM THE MODEL OF A GREAT METROPOLIS

KENNETH T. JACKSON

In 1964, when the World's Fair opened in Flushing Meadows Corona Park in the borough of Queens, New York was unique among cities. By every test of economic and cultural significance applicable to urban centers, it was in a class alone. Its municipal population of more than seven million was larger than any other place, as was its metropolitan total of thirteen million. New York led the planet in manufacturing, wholesale and retail trade, advertising, finance, banking, communication, insurance, and engineering. The metropolitan region included more than a quarter of the country's designers, 18 percent of its attorneys and judges, and more than 15 percent of accountants, architects, chemists, and electrical engineers. Almost half of the nation's waterborne commerce, measured by dollar value, flowed through its vast harbor. It was the hub of an enormous transportation network with three major airports and eleven railroads reaching out in all directions. As the home of the United Nations, it was, in a real sense, the capital of the world.

In general, unless one spends thousands of dollars to rent a helicopter for an aerial tour of the five boroughs, most people will have no way of grasping the geographical, architectural, and transportation complexity of this most developed of cities. Most New Yorkers just follow our everyday routes through the familiar subways, roads, and sidewalks, and notice the structures and places that we see along our way. But we have no real way of understanding the unusual human agglomeration in which we live.

The Panorama of the City of New York gives us insights we would otherwise never have. There is nothing quite like it on any of the planet's seven continents. What exactly are the benefits of a visit to the *Panorama*? Having led groups to the facility for more than thirty years, I will offer just a partial list of its wondrous examples.

First, visitors will notice the importance of water. Indeed, all great cities—London, Paris, Tokyo, Mumbai, Kolkata, Singapore, Hong Kong, Rio de Janeiro, Buenos Aires, Moscow, St. Petersburg, Amsterdam, Berlin, Budapest, Stockholm, Rome, Milan, Istanbul, Shanghai, Chicago, Los Angeles, San Francisco, and São Paulo among them—are located on navigable water. The few exceptions—Mexico City, Lagos, Dallas, and Atlanta—simply prove the point.

The *Panorama* reveals how dependent the five boroughs are upon water. For example, while the rivers of most world cities are human scale and easily crossed by small bridges, the bays and rivers of New York Harbor are wide and the bridges that allow persons to get to the other side are necessarily large. At the time of their construction, the Brooklyn Bridge, the George Washington Bridge, and the Verrazzano-Narrows Bridge were the largest such structures in the world. So, while it is easy for lovers to stroll across the waterways of London, Paris, Berlin, Amsterdam, and Moscow,

casual strollers are unusual on the Verrazzano-Narrows or George Washington Bridges. Most important, the Brooklyn Bridge has always provided a matchless vantage point from which to view the busy East River below. As famed urbanist Lewis Mumford remembered the scene: "Here was my city, immense, overpowering, flooded with energy and light; there below lay the river and the harbor, catching the last flakes of gold on their waters, with the black tugs, free from their barges, plodding dockward, the ferry boats lumbering from pier to pier, the tramp steamers slowly crawling toward the sea."

Second, the land abutting the waterfront is phenomenal in terms of its length. By far the longest urban shoreline in the United States, that of the city and northeastern New Jersey runs 770 miles. It is one of the largest natural harbors in the world. There were times during World War II when several hundred ships could be at wharfs and piers around the city *at the same time*. As late as the 1950s, the west side of Manhattan, from the Battery up to at least 52nd Street, was lined with piers, warehouses, garbage dumps, and terminals; and the Hudson and East Rivers were crowded with tramp steamers, ferries, lighters (small barges with railroad freight cars on them), sailboats, and ocean liners. The East River was narrower than the Hudson, but also crowded with maritime shipping of every variety. And although it is not obvious from the *Panorama*, LaGuardia and JFK airports, plus that of Newark, make the metropolis the nation's top gateway for international flights.

Another dramatic visual impression from the *Panorama* is the 6,000 skyscrapers in New York, most of them in lower and Midtown Manhattan, and the general absence of such structures in the outer boroughs. The tall buildings are mostly unique, each unlike other skyscrapers. Some are architecturally notable, such as Mies van der Rohe's Seagram Building (1958) or Philip Johnson and John Burgee's Lipstick Building (1986), but the overall impression is of difference. One can easily distinguish the United Nations complex on the *Panorama*, which symbolizes the emergence of New York as the capital of the world.

The original *Panorama* also underscores the concentration of so-called "towers in the park," a model of public housing that emphasized buildings of at least ten stories surrounded by open spaces with playgrounds, walkways, extensive greenery, and parking lots for residents. We realized too late that such projects were repetitive, numbing, red brick monstrosities that imposed a mazelike and soulless anonymity on living conditions for individuals with low income. The New York City government built 75,000 such units (40,000 of them in Harlem) before Robert Moses resigned from his chairman position in the Mayor's Committee of Slum Clearance in 1960. By the end of the decade the municipality was landlord to more than 500,000 low-income residents. The *Panorama* reveals a few such New York concentrations, such as Parkchester and Co-op City in the Bronx, Stuyvesant Town and Peter Cooper Village in Manhattan, and Starrett City in Brooklyn, but they do not dominate any borough.

Another major icon on the *Panorama* is Central Park. Observers notice both the enormous size and the central location of the world's most important public open space. This great urban park comprises 843 acres in the middle of what would become the most expensive real estate anywhere. A half mile wide and two-and-a-half miles long, the park is surrounded by tall buildings on every side, many of them both enormous and famous.

Even in a city that revolves around—more than any other city in the nation—public transit and walking, the *Panorama* suggests that the automobile remains paramount. Moses masterminded the construction of more than 600 miles of highways and, increasingly in the 1950s, six-lane expressways. Perhaps the most infamous (and visible on the *Panorama*) was the seven-mile-long Cross Bronx Expressway that ran through the middle of a neighborhood called East Tremont along the northern edge of Crotona Park. Although residents organized many protests against the road and even mapped out alternative routes, Moses was unmoved. By 1955, nine years after Moses had first proposed his idea, the city

Central Park, Manhattan, *The Panorama of the City of New York*, 2016. Digital photograph. © Max Touhey.

Aerial view, looking north-east over Manhattan, *The Panorama of the City of New York,* **ca. 1994.** Vintage silver gelatin print.

Left
Removal of the "helicopter" ride in *The Panorama of the City of New York* during the 1992–94 restoration, ca. 1992. Vintage silver gelatin print. © Phyllis Bilick.

Below
Worker detailing Staten Island on *The Panorama of the City of New York* during the 1992–94 restoration, ca. 1993. Scanned 35mm slide.

government had already displaced almost 60,000 inhabitants. In 1963, the expressway opened.

Finally, what most visitors will remember most vividly after departing from the *Panorama* is the vast size of the city of New York. The largest of the five boroughs, Queens, is almost as large as the Bronx, Manhattan, and Staten Island combined. As you look over Queens, Staten Island, Brooklyn, and the Bronx, you can see just how large and how sprawling the great city is.

Changes in the City and the Model between 1964 and 1994

In 1992, the *Panorama* was completely closed for two years so that workers from Lester Associates could update the original model. They eliminated the "helicopter"-style conveyances that had carried visitors over the model. They added 60,000 new structures (for a new total of almost 900,000 model buildings) as well as an elevated walkway that allowed visitors to linger over favorite sites for the first time.

Of the hundreds of new projects that took shape between 1964 and 1994, five have special significance. The first is the gigantic World Trade Center (WTC) complex. Developed by the Port Authority of New York and New Jersey, the site was spearheaded by David Rockefeller, chairman of the Chase Manhattan Bank and allegedly the second most powerful person in the nation at the time. The sixteen-acre site was originally proposed for the east side of lower Manhattan. New Jersey objected, and so the new location was the former "Radio Row" on the lower west side of Manhattan. After the eviction of 323 commercial or industrial tenants, construction on the North Tower began in August 1968, and on the South Tower in 1969. The buildings went up quickly, opening in 1970 and 1972, and cost what would now be $15 billion. They had, among other things, 43,600 windows, 23,000 fluorescent lights, and 194 elevators between the two towers. Four other structures were added in 1973, and a seventh structure, 7 World Trade Center, opened in 1987.

Ultimately, the WTC site encompassed more than 15 million square feet of office space, making it larger than the Pentagon, which had previously been sanctioned as the world's largest office building. For the next quarter century, the Twin Towers helped define New York City. They crowned the skyline and helped citizens in many areas determine their sense of direction. Each was a full acre straight up, and they sparked a cultural, residential, and commercial revival in lower Manhattan.

The Panorama Gallery, north view, after *The Panorama of the City of New York* had been removed for renovations, November 17, 1992. Vintage silver gelatin print. © Phil di Domenico.

The Financial District, Manhattan, *The Panorama of the City of New York,* **ca. 1970s.** Vintage silver gelatin print.

Every visitor to the *Panorama* will know that the Twin Towers were destroyed on September 11, 2001, when two huge airliners, each loaded with jet fuel for scheduled flights to the West Coast, were hijacked by terrorists who intentionally crashed them into the two 110-story skyscrapers. Within two hours, both buildings had collapsed, killing more than 2,750 people and unleashing a scene of previously unimaginable destruction. Yet, despite the complete obliteration of the World Trade Center on September 11, the *Panorama* features the giant complex as it originally stood. There is a new and even taller structure on the site today, but the *Panorama* shows you the WTC as it was.

Near the World Trade Center is Battery Park City, another major alteration to the city occurring during the *Panorama*'s lifetime. It is a predominantly residential community on ninety-two acres of landfill in what used to be dilapidated shipping piers in the Hudson River. The area had once been a busy seaport, but the rise of container shipping moved most activity to the New Jersey side. Meanwhile, the whole shoreline on the lower west side went into steep decline. In 1968, however, the New York State Legislature created the Battery Park City Authority to remove the old piers. Landfill from the World Trade Center and other buildings added to the available space. The complex had not been completed at the time the *Panorama* reopened in 1994, but was subsequently added.

Another impactful mutation to the built environment of New York, and one that is clearly visible on the *Panorama*, is Lincoln Center for the Performing Arts. Generally regarded as the most concentrated and important cultural site in the world, it is a

Detail, the World Trade Center, Manhattan, *The Panorama of the City of New York*, ca. 1974–77. Scanned 35mm slide. Anonymous gift.

Detail, the Statue of Liberty with the World Trade Center in the background, Manhattan, *The Panorama of the City of New York*, 2004. Digital photograph. © Eileen Costa.

sixteen-acre complex of buildings that together attract more than five million visitors every year. The largest of them is the Metropolitan Opera House, which has the most seating (3,900) and the biggest budget of any such institution anywhere. Among the thirty indoor and outdoor facilities are the New York Philharmonic's David Geffen Hall (formerly Avery Fisher Hall), the New York City Ballet's David H. Koch Theater, the Juilliard School, Alice Tully Hall, the Vivian Beaumont Theater, and Jazz at Lincoln Center.

Many people helped make Lincoln Center happen. The first name that comes to mind is John D. Rockefeller III, who became the first chairman of the complex in 1955 and later served as chairman and chief fundraiser for Lincoln Center. Other critical players included the mighty Robert Moses, who alienated thousands of neighborhood residents by demolishing hundreds of older structures in the area under a contentious urban renewal program; and President Dwight Eisenhower, who presided at the groundbreaking ceremony in 1959. In 1964, the first of the major buildings, the New York State Theater, opened, joined by the Vivian Beaumont Theater and the Metropolitan Opera in 1965, and the Juilliard School and Alice Tully Hall in 1969.

Midtown Manhattan, *The Panorama of the City of New York,* **1994.** Digital photograph. © Laila Bahman/BFAnyc

The North River Wastewater Treatment Plant, a giant construction project that occurred after the *Panorama*'s debut, was another significant change that we can now consider in the updated model. Built on new land in the Hudson River along the Henry Hudson Parkway between 137th Street and 145th Street on the Upper West Side, the sewage plant was constructed in 1985. However, what is not included is Riverbank State Park, the impressive park built on top, which opened in 1993. The twenty-eight-acre complex is now replete with basketball courts, an Olympic-size swimming pool, a covered skating rink for ice skating in the winter and roller skating in the summer, playgrounds, soccer fields, tennis courts, community gardens, and baseball diamonds. It even supports trees of up to thirty-five feet tall in some areas. As one of only three state parks within Manhattan, it has been an enormous success and still treats 340 million gallons of wastewater per day.

The largest construction project that changed the city between 1964 and 1994 was Co-op City in the Bronx. The area was mostly marshland and was partially occupied by a 205-acre amusement park called Freedomland USA from 1960 to 1964. It was modeled on the Disneyland concept in southern California, but it was a financial failure. In February 1965, plans were announced for Co-op City: the builder would be the United Housing Foundation, an organization established in 1951 by Abraham Kazan and the Amalgamated Clothing Workers of America; the architect was Herman J. Jessor.

Construction of Co-op City began in May 1966, and the first residents began moving in before the end of 1968. All construction was completed in 1973. Ultimately, the complex included thirty-five skyscrapers from twenty-six to thirty-three stories, as well as seven clusters of 236 three-story townhouses. It remains the largest cooperative housing development in American history. Ultimately, this city within a city offered residents a high school, two middle schools, three grade schools, six nursery schools, four basketball courts, five baseball diamonds, a shopping center, a multiplex movie theater, several department stores, and a supermarket. Co-op City can easily be seen on the *Panorama* where Interstate 95 and the Hutchinson River Parkway bisect the complex in the northeast part of the Bronx. It occupies 320 acres and houses more than 40,000 residents.

These five major projects do not, of course, completely account for the transformation of the *Panorama* between 1964 and 1994.

In those three decades, the skyline itself changed. In the 1960s tall buildings of Manhattan were essentially concentrated in the middle of the island and along the north–south route of Fifth Avenue. The skyscrapers made the island resemble a wedding cake, with a tall center and much lower edges. By the 1990s the East and Hudson River waterfronts were beginning to experience redevelopment in the vicinity of the shoreline that would dramatically change the city in the twenty-first century.

There are many reasons for the transformation of New York in the quarter century after the first model was built. Perhaps most important was the spectacular decline of factory and industrial jobs and the corresponding growth of legal and financial services. Meanwhile, federal legislation in 1965 made it easier for immigrants to come to America. So many of them came to America that, by 2000, the five boroughs had almost three million documented, foreign-born residents. Meanwhile, a new private initiative called the Central Park Conservancy returned the once great open space to its former glory. Times Square began to focus on grandmothers with their granddaughters and tourists rather than drug dealers, prostitutes, and peep shows. And Mayor Edward Koch, who served three terms from 1978 until 1990, helped convince skeptics that the great city was, in fact, governable. Abandoned buildings and factories in industrial areas, especially in Harlem, Williamsburg, Sunset Park, Fort Greene, and Long Island City, began to gentrify.

The Transformation of New York City since the *Panorama* Update in 1994

The most striking thing about the metropolis since 1994 has been the continued growth and building of the city. Most visibly, there are now tall buildings along the lower west side of Manhattan, along the east side of Riverside Drive above 72nd Street, and in Brooklyn along the East River—but that is just scratching the surface. Millions of residents and tourists are drawn to a once-decrepit elevated freight railroad that has been converted into a world-class attraction called the High Line, which runs from 38th Street south almost to Jane Street. This is an example of how New York is always changing but always offering excitement, diversity, and energy.

Queens, Roosevelt Island,
and Manhattan, with the
Ed Koch Queensboro Bridge,
*The Panorama of the City of
New York*, 2004.

Digital photograph. © Eileen Costa.

MAP COLOR CODE

- Local roads
- Highways and parkways
- Urban blocks
- City blocks
- Parks
- Cemeteries
- Transportation depots
- Sections outside city limits
- Publicly subsidized housing
- Recreational areas
  playgrounds, tennis courts, basketball courts, baseball fields, etc.

MUNICIPAL RESOURCES

In 1964, the top twelve most prevalent types of facilities run by the City were:

Parks and recreational centers: 1,991

Schools (elementary, high school, college): 870

Sanitation departments: 265

Fire departments: 251

Welfare centers: 291

Libraries: 186

Public housing: 131

Police precincts: 123

Health centers and hospitals: 113

Courts and penal institutions: 53

Museums: 25

Water, gas, and electric facilities: 20

According to Lester Associates' research

Right

Panels of *The Panorama of the City of New York* being moved out of the Queens Museum in advance of the 1992–94 restoration.

Vintage silver gelatin print.

Below

Handling roads to be placed in Queens on *The Panorama of the City of New York* during the 1992–94 restoration, ca. 1993.

Scanned 35mm slide.

The Bronx and Upper Manhattan being removed from the Panorama Gallery in advance of the 1992–94 restoration, ca. 1992.

Scanned 35mm slide.

Worker detailing the Old Mill
Basin neighborhood of Queens on
*The Panorama of the City of New
York* during the 1992–94
restoration, ca. 1993.

Scanned 35mm slide.

Top

Worker detailing the Brighton Beach neighborhood of Brooklyn on *The Panorama of the City of New York* during the 1992–94 restoration, ca. 1993.

Scanned 35mm slide.

Bottom

Worker doing paint touch-ups on a panel of *The Panorama of the City of New York* during the 1992–94 restoration, ca. 1993.

Scanned 35mm slide.

Above

**Maintenance of *The Panorama
of the City of New York*, ca. 1980.**

Vintage silver gelatin print.

Right

**Cleaning *The Panorama of the
City of New York*, ca. 1994.**

Vintage silver gelatin print.
© Phyllis Bilick.

A BUILDING ENVIRONMENT: *THE PANORAMA OF THE CITY OF NEW YORK*

A CONVERSATION WITH VALERIE PALEY AND VYJAYANTHI RAO

EDITED BY LYNN MALISZEWSKI

Lynn Maliszewski: Are there elements of social existence in New York City that you wish could be visualized on *The Panorama of the City of New York*?

Valerie Paley: I don't even know where to begin when pondering the *Panorama*. You can contemplate it as an object, awesome in scale, charming in its dollhouse quality, accuracy, and detail. It might be stuck in 1992, when it was last updated, but what one doesn't see is the cultural fabric of the neighborhoods. You can recognize the outlines of the Commissioners' Plan of 1811,[1] which tamed the natural landscape for development, but we don't detect any people or get a larger sense of how density impacts the way they live in this city. Right now on display at New-York Historical Society is the Castello Plan, the earliest known map of New York when it was still New Amsterdam. A video model allows you to virtually tour the streets in a way that has a fascinating resonance: the DNA of the city seems to be embedded in those lanes and alleyways from the 1660s. The mercantile character of the Dutch metropolis morphs into something more corporate in feeling, three hundred years later, in the *Panorama*.

Vyjayanthi Rao: For me, part of the interesting thing about the *Panorama* is that it is really space without time, space outside of time. Can we think about culture also in those terms? Of course I don't think we can because it's constantly evolving, it's constantly changing. If you think about the historical character of neighborhoods, even as they were thirty years ago and how different they are today, it's actually a formidable problem for representation. How do you get time and space into a visual object or visual medium that has dimensionality? I would like to think a little bit about that also because I think art has played such a huge role in New York City, and in its transformation, in its gentrification, and there's so many intertwined aspects to the way the city is represented, represents itself, and the way that its people, its demographics, are constantly altering the landscape.

Perhaps one interesting way to think about how to represent time and the transformation of neighborhoods in the *Panorama* is to look at the alterations that different communities or different groups have made to that plan. I was jaywalking yesterday, for example, in New Haven [Connecticut] and the person I was with was talking about, *Oh, so now we do the dumb diagonal?* There's this really weird system of diagonals where the lights never seem to turn green, and it occurred to me that I was just going to disregard one of those lights and walk across in a diagonal fashion and create my own sidewalk. I think that's a lot of what New Yorkers do in terms of how they make space in the city. It's always striking when you see the *Panorama* that these thoughts come immediately

to you: it's a fantastic representation but it's almost unreal and surreal because it's not how we inhabit the city with our bodies.

Valerie Paley: It's a sculptural representation of the city's built environment for sure, but what's missing is the humanity, the transactions of the people who navigate that built environment. How does that influence our understanding of the place? I find myself thinking as much about the argument for creating the *Panorama* in the first place—promoting an idea of progress, celebrating three hundred years of New York in 1964—and now, on a purely literal level, thinking, *well, look what's not here . . . Long Island City's not here, the bike lanes are not here, the High Line's not there.* And do those new, missing things capture something important about the city's present and future? Without those places, does the *Panorama* become just a very quaint artifact of the past, versus a more visceral illustration of what the city is?

How is it that in such a dense metropolis, certain people who are mortal enemies elsewhere on the planet somehow coexist and manage to ride the subway together without incident? We don't see that kind of nuance in the *Panorama*. How do the people who call themselves New Yorkers impact the spirit of the city? And how does that change over time? There are some historians who would say that because New Amsterdam was founded by the Dutch as a locus for making money, as opposed to a religious haven, mercantilism is embedded in the city's continuing character.

Vyjayanthi Rao: I'm so provoked to think about these ideas. If we add in certain artifacts of the recent past, what kind of city do they represent? You're right that if we take the bike lanes and the High Line and add those in, then we get an idea that there is some consciousness of nature, of ecology, and perhaps consciousness that is driven by the crisis mode that the city finds itself in. The other interesting point you made is that there's secular foundations of a mercantile city, which allowed the founders at least to disregard certain principles in the generation of new modes of dealing with a city. So what are the artifacts that we need to add in?

Could we think about crisis as a moment of truth for cities that are founded on highly transactional, secular principles? Where there are no even or steady values as such—apart from the fact that there's a maximization of profit for everyone, including the poorest of the immigrants—why do people live in certain conditions which one would think are not really acceptable to human dignity? The reason is because they're better off here, somehow, than they would be in other places. One of the things that makes me really proud to be a New Yorker is the fact that this is a sanctuary city, and somehow it's held on to that, or tried to. But that's, again, a crisis for the city, as we've seen new migrants arriving in the last year. So, with this *Panorama*, how can we stretch the idea of what we add in to represent those moments or those turning points that can then tell us what comes next or who are the people that will shape [it]? Even if we can't put the humans in the *Panorama*, I think we can use these artifacts to gauge what might be the demographic shift, the ethos, the shift of the ethos of the citizens as such.

Valerie Paley: Exactly: how can the *Panorama* possibly capture the lives of the millions of people living in New York? I find it fascinating that this object was touted as a representation of a "range of human achievements." In 1964, it showed a range of Robert Moses's achievements, not necessarily "human" achievement. The original light cycles, for example, show city services, which are more institutional than human: protection, education, health, recreation, welfare, transportation. It's a very large picture of what a city can be. I'm struck by the difference between the points of view of Moses versus Jane Jacobs,[2] who saw city planning on a much more intimate, personal level.

Vyjayanthi Rao: In this virtual age, I think it's worth thinking about what that dimensionality can teach us, or tell us, about how we experience the city—through all our senses, not just visually, which is what we've become so attuned to in a very short period of time in our history. Drone photography, which can represent the aerial point of view in a very different but realistic way, is a fascinating contrast because, regardless of what the *Panorama* represents, there's a visceral quality to its being a physical object. When we see hyperrealistic aerial drone images, they actually tell us even less than the *Panorama* does about what's happening or how to feel, or how to experience. So that's an aspect of the *Panorama* that stands out for me even more now; it has this power to shake you up. I would not expect that with a drone shot.

I want to pick up on what you mentioned, Valerie, about institutions and the fact that highlighting institutions is so important. I wonder if we can think about other forms of civic institutions that are equally vital today that don't find any space on the *Panorama*. Going back to the COVID era, there was a lot of guerrilla infrastructure being created by people to fill in the gaps of what they were not getting at the time, which made some super beautiful uses of space, vacant spaces—creating composting sites, all kinds of mutual aid distribution centers, restaurant clusters, and then the sidewalk cafés and all of that. That human infrastructure was all part of the built environment.

Valerie Paley: Absolutely. The city services the *Panorama* focused upon touch just about everything: "Protection" like fire, police, traffic, corrections, courts; "Education," covering the libraries, the schools, the museums, the colleges; "Health," including water, gas, electricity; "Recreation," parks, beaches, playgrounds; and "Welfare and Transportation," essentially housing and roadways. There's nothing wrong with that, which exactly categorizes what the *Panorama* shows, but it does it in an excruciatingly bureaucratic way. With that approach, though, how could you ever account for the shifts in daily life that happened during COVID, for example, which took place on a more private level?

Vyjayanthi Rao: I think this combination of being able to look from above and also feel oneself in the space can also give people who have never been [to New York] an uncanny Proustian experience, like déjà vu of an experience that you never had. Which is kind of, in my case, what I first felt when I went to London because of having grown up in India and being so familiar with the city through English literature from certain periods. I almost knew the streets of London before I got there. I think that the *Panorama* has that power to give us an experience that we maybe never had, a memory of some kind even if it is a bureaucratically arranged and ordained one.

Valerie Paley: Growing up in Greenwich Village—where one still can have a somewhat palpable sense of what New York might have been like in the nineteenth century—I had that imaginary, retrospective, Proustian sense of what it might have been like to walk up and down those streets, climb those stoops, and project myself into another time in that very place. I remember always defending the city to out-of-towners, whose whole experience or impression of the city was the squalor of Times Square or the disorderly approach to the airport. They couldn't comprehend my semi-romantic sense of New York because "progress" plowed over the natural landscape and demolished the structures of prior centuries. Even as the *Panorama* captured Robert Moses's vision of progress in the 1960s, simultaneously there was the beginning of the Landmarks Preservation Movement—progress of a different sort. The bridges and all the infrastructural elements of the city are in place, but the more micro-human elements, which might be articulated by historic buildings or neighborhoods, were evidently not important in this scenario. Any kind of deep thinking about the *Panorama* triggers so much about the competing urban planning visions of Moses and Jane Jacobs.

Vyjayanthi Rao: I agree that it's really a provocation to think about what is invisible, and what is unseen. One of the students I taught at City College in fall 2020, during a semester that was very much intertwined with the Queens Museum and the *Panorama*, was interested in alterations of the built environment that

The Panorama of the City of New York, 2004. Digital photograph. © Eileen Costa.

are widespread but invisible: basements and subdivisions within buildings. In the course of his research, he realized that while these alterations are invisible in some ways and for obvious reasons, they could become visible if one knows how to look. So his method, his way in, was to look at building violations, and then create a map of these alterations through those instances where violations had happened. It was very telling because there's a provocation there: you use that information to get underneath the surface or into those structures and see what *might* be happening. The more this conversation progresses, the more attached I get to this idea of having this huge, unwieldy object that can serve so many different purposes apart from the one that was originally envisioned.

Valerie Paley: How cool would it be to see what's been lost or what's going on just under the surface—what the city looked like before contact, or what it looked like in the nineteenth century? To take different snapshots in time—aspects of the city's history and demography—and layer them over this particular object could be a profound historical and planning teaching tool, maybe even an anthropological tool as well. How many people lived in those neighborhoods? What went on in those buildings?

I was in the Financial District earlier this week and reminiscing about how, not too long ago, after work closed up at six, seven o'clock, there was *nobody* there. You went to work and then you went home somewhere else. Not anymore! How can the *Panorama* depict that kind of change in the vibrancy of a locale that physically looks about the same as it did twenty, thirty, forty years ago, but has a very different character now? It's the same for parts of Brooklyn, Queens, Staten Island. Think of how technology might enable us to see the many alterations and the disruptions, both physically and culturally.

Vyjayanthi Rao: One of the ideas that came to mind is the archeological nature of this artifact. In any city that has existed for a certain length of time, you will find that there is some kind of archeological base from which you can read its DNA in some way. Maybe the same mistakes keep getting repeated in relation to the same sort of natural artifacts, or things that cannot be changed.

Almost a year after Hurricane Sandy, I was living in lower Manhattan and Peter, a Dutch anthropologist friend of mine, had come to visit. He wanted to take a walk to the [East] River so we went up to Front Street and stood near the shore. Peter had this absolutely horrified look on his face. I sort of understood at that moment what he was thinking: *I bet the Dutch would have never done this.* Suddenly a lightbulb went off and I thought, *yes, I believe that.* Everything from Front Street to the FDR [Drive] actually came much later. So I said, "Don't worry, it wasn't a Dutch mistake." It seemed like he immediately perceived that, coming from Amsterdam and being in "New Amsterdam," the shoreline should not have been so vulnerable. The geology and archeology of the city actually builds in clues regarding this intense transactionality, this environmental disregard, this idea that technology can conquer everything and make everything even for all time. But then, as we know, crisis after crisis, decade on decade, there's been something that has altered the fabric of the city in such a fundamental way, and we are still not able to represent it.

Valerie Paley: In terms of the geology and geography, I've encountered some New Yorkers who don't even realize they live on an island. You certainly see that you *are*, when you're standing over the *Panorama*. But you may not grasp that so much of lower Manhattan and its shoreline are built on landfill. I'm charmed by streets in the Seaport area that are "slips"—they were literally slips where ships docked. How ecologically sound is that, and how arrogant was it to pave it over and build on it?

Worker in the Lester Associates workshop consulting an aerial photograph of New York City, ca. 1963. Scanned 35mm negative. Gift of Lester Associates.

There would be some New York historians who would say that idea, indeed, might be consistent with our Dutch heritage because that's all about maximizing profits. But the Dutch today might counter that they would have had at least a little bit more sense about how to do it, how to use the geography of the place to make it work. When I think about crisis in New York, the fiscal crisis of the 1970s also comes to mind. It's not an environmental crisis, but it did impact the city in serious ways. By some accounts, it was the nadir of the city, the worst time in its history, and yet, so many important artistic and cultural contributions were happening in a moment when the urban landscape was in a state of decay.

Vyjayanthi Rao: That moment of financial crisis drove people out of the city. It was also very profoundly related to race and the racialization of the inner city and its consequent neglect. The corresponding growth of the suburbs, which became the places that people went to when they went home, meant that downtown was just a place to work. The return of downtown is a completely different environment, and also has some other implications that have to do culturally with how people think about work and life. This built environment has now become a 24/7 environment: it's where you live, where you work, where everything is happening. What can we do with the *Panorama* to represent that? In one way, it is

Downtown Manhattan, *The Panorama of the City of New York*, ca. 1980. Scanned large-format color positive film.

Manhattan, Queens, and Brooklyn, *The Panorama of the City of New York*, 2016. Digital photograph. © Max Touhey.

vibrant; in another way, it produces a great deal of anxiety around what our lives are about. Are we tethered to continuous productivity or a machine that is extracting our labor all the time? *American Psycho*, for example, is set in that same landscape. This is the incredible correlation between looking at or being in or reading the built environment.

Valerie Paley: Right, and how do you demonstrate how it's *not* characterized? There's a built environment, but who lives in that environment? And how have shifting demographics changed the nature of the place, the culture of the place, the soul of the place?

Lynn Maliszewski: I want to come back to dimensionality: how does the *Panorama* as a static synopsis of the city at a moment in time rest alongside the fact that the city is in constant flux?

Valerie Paley: I think the flux is embedded in the people: who they are, culturally and physically; what they do; what the city represents to them. You can't really see that kind of change in the built environment of the *Panorama*. For the longest time, certain streets of New York, of Manhattan in particular, stood in for larger cultural things: Seventh Avenue, fashion; Fifth Avenue, great wealth; Madison Avenue, advertising; Wall Street, merchants and trading. We see those thoroughfares in the *Panorama*, but we don't have a sense of what goes on there. It's not that those particular things have changed, but the people who are engaged in those activities have changed a great deal.

Marking streets on *The Panorama of the City of New York* **in the Lester Associates workshop, ca. 1962. Scanned 35mm negative. Gift of Lester Associates.**

Rack of standardized building pieces for *The Panorama of the City of New York* in the Lester Associates workshop, ca. 1963. Scanned 35mm negative. Gift of Lester Associates.

Vyjayanthi Rao: I was thinking that instead of using the phrase "built environment," which kind of suggests a process that's finished, maybe we can replace it with "a building environment," which actually incorporates a physical aspect of structures that have been completed, on the one hand, but also the past that's embedded in those streets and the flux that is part of the apparently finished. So even if the people have changed, somehow they buttress the basic elements to build something else or take it somewhere else.

When I look at Hudson Yards, for example, it's like an alien spaceship because it is not part of the built environment that is being adapted. It's really something that's been dropped in, and it represents a radically different imaginary, even visually. That environment will give rise to a very different form of building culture or building community than will the rest of what we've inherited from the past. I'm reading N. K. Jemisin, who makes New York City her canvas. It makes me think how a lot of sci-fi also draws on the past coming back in a very visceral way. The stories of the past are just flooding into spaces that have been totally transformed by capital, by people. That's just a way of thinking about shifting from the built environment as a past object to an environment for building, turning it into "a building environment," or a building block.

Valerie Paley: I like the word *building*, too, because here we're not talking about a physical thing; it's the idea of building something more, like building a culture.

Vyjayanthi Rao: The *Panorama* can enable us to do that, as a situated platform for building. When we think about cities as static, we forget how much maintenance, how much care, it takes to keep them standing. I think that is an aspect that somehow has to come into this *Panorama* narrative because it's also the narrative of the feminine, of the domestic. How can one imagine a different kind of economy that is not based on complete exploitation and extraction, but instead on caring, maintaining, keeping something upright, keeping the built from becoming unbuilt? That also alludes to a different kind of demographic that is more or less invisible. The *Panorama* really highlights the civic institutions that are state-built and corporate-built, and that require enormous amounts of financial or fiscal maintenance. But then there's this whole other kind of labor that everything else requires.

Worker at Lester Associates paints buildings on a template for *The Panorama of the City of New York*, ca. 1963. Scanned 35mm slide. Gift of Lester Associates.

Valerie Paley: That makes me think of how the smaller buildings in the *Panorama* are not as well detailed and are likely older. When one sees a very ordinary nineteenth-century building with beautiful ornamentation we have to remember the European immigrant artisans and workers who applied a particular capacity, skill, and aesthetic to their work. We generally don't bother to embellish ordinary buildings that way anymore. What prompts those kinds of decisions about the built or building environment? Post-COVID, we're accustomed to a different way of functioning in general. We adapted. The *Panorama* sparks a philosophical contemplation of how we live in this space.

This conversation was held via Zoom on April 19, 2024.

1. In 1811, the New York State Legislature convened a commission to lay out roads, streets, and public space in a rectilinear grid system, from Houston Street to 155th Street. This plan was intended to make the expansion of infrastructure, transportation, and housing for Manhattan's growing population more efficient and effective.
2. Robert Moses and Jane Jacobs are emblematic of two very different sets of values when it comes to city planning and infrastructure. Moses, lauded as "the master builder" after a decades-long career in city government, prioritized the ease of transport via automobile to the suburbs and infrastructure that facilitated that movement. Jacobs was an urbanist and activist, seeking to preserve the density, diversity, and accessibility of the city for all inhabitants through protest and written critiques of Moses-era policies and transformations.

Manhattan, Brooklyn, and
Governors Island, *The Panorama
of the City of New York*, 2016.
Digital photograph. © Max Touhey

Right
The Panorama of the City of New York, 2015.
Digital photograph. © Max Touhey.

Overleaf
Queens, looking southwest, *The Panorama of the City of New York, 2015.*
Digital photograph. © Max Touhey.

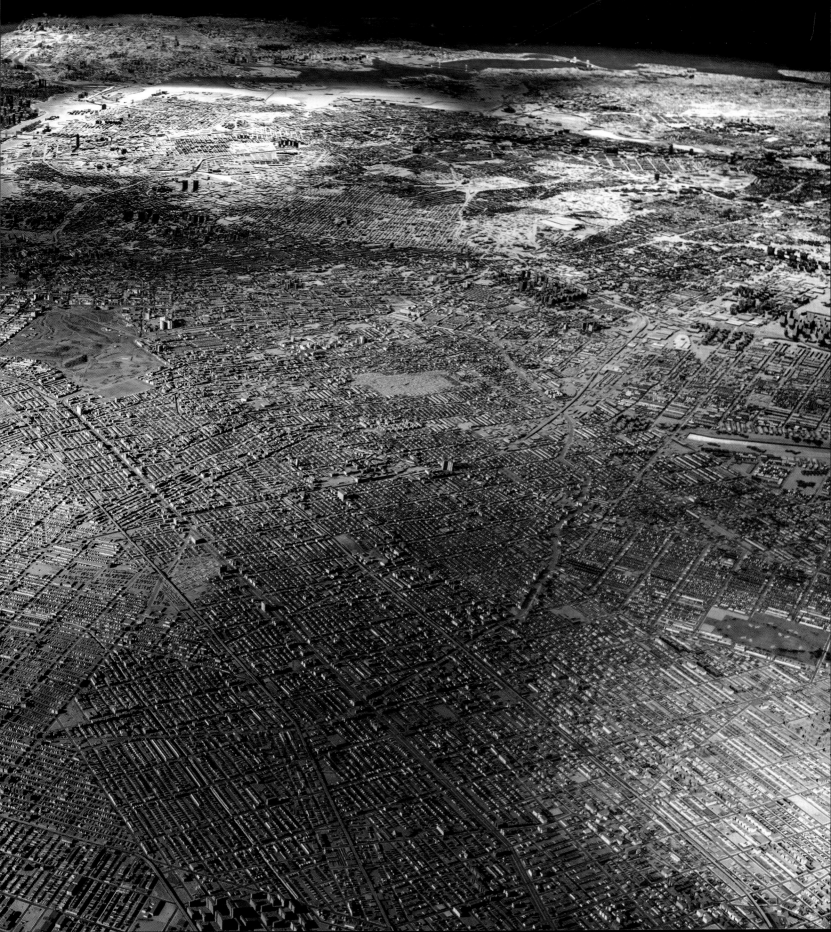

HOW BIG IS THE PANORAMA?

Length at the longest point:

154 feet 6 inches from the Bronx city line at Westchester to the tip of Staten Island at Perth Amboy

Width at the widest point:

137 feet from the west side of Manhattan to the Nassau County line

Approximate borough sizes:

**Manhattan: 70 × 15 feet
The Bronx: 40 × 40 feet
Brooklyn: 50 × 50 feet
Queens: 60 × 75 feet
Staten Island: 50 × 70 feet**

Landmarks:

Statue of Liberty
1⅛ inches tall, 3¼ inches tall (including base)

Central Park
27¾ × 135¼ inches

Verrazzano-Narrows Bridge
71½ × 1 inches, tower height is 7 inches

One Court Square (formerly Citicorp)
6¾ inches tall

Brooklyn Bridge
41¼ × 1 inches, tower height is 3 inches

George Washington Bridge
48 × 1¹⁄₁₆ inches, tower height is 6 inches

Staten Island Ferry route
264 inches

Coney Island Beach
160¼ inches

Queens Museum
4½ × 2⅛ inches, height is ½ inch

Empire State Building
15 inches

Above

Flushing Meadows Corona Park, Queens, *The Panorama of the City of New York*, 2004.

Digital photograph. © Eileen Scott.

Right

Coney Island, Brooklyn, *The Panorama of the City of New York*, 2004.

Digital photograph. © Eileen Costa.

Manhattan, *The Panorama of the City of New York*, 2016.
Digital photograph. © Max Touhey.

The Verrazzano-Narrows Bridge,
The Panorama of the City of New York, ca. 1964.

Vintage silver gelatin print. Gift of
Lester Associates.

LIGHTING CYCLES

3,172 colored lights appeared on the original *Panorama*, showing the location of municipal facilities in five discrete cycles:

Protection cycle:

- **Fire departments**
- **Police departments**
- **Traffic departments**
- **Department of Corrections**
- **New York City courts**

Education cycle:

- **Public libraries**
- **Elementary schools**
- **Museums and historical institutions**
- **High schools**
- **Colleges**

Health cycle:

● **Water, gas, and electric**

● **Additional city services**

● **Department of Health**

○ **Department of Sanitation**

○ **Department of Hospitals**

Recreation cycle:

● **Recreation buildings**

● **Golf courses**

● **Parks**

○ **Beaches**

○ **Playgrounds**

Commerce, Welfare, and Transportation cycle:

● **Department of Transportation**

● **Department of Welfare**

● **Housing Authority**

○ **Department of Marine & Aviation**

○ **City office structures**

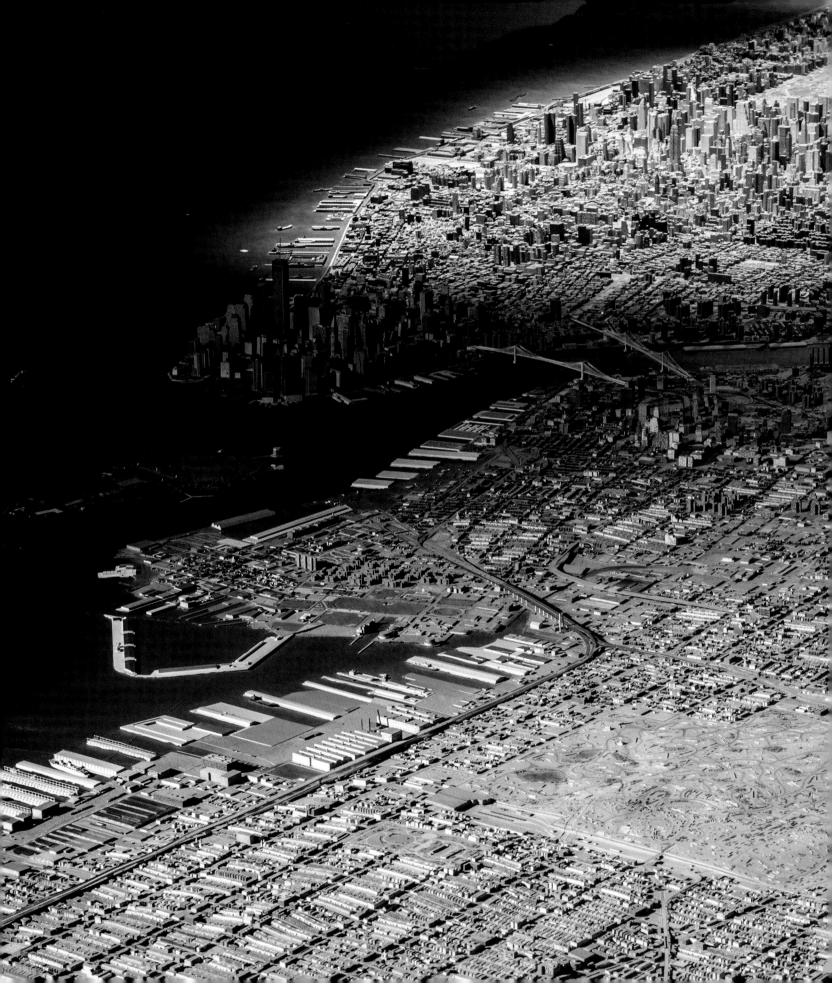

Brooklyn, looking northwest
toward Manhattan, *The
Panorama of the City of New
York*, 2016.

Digital photograph. © Max Touhey.

Right

Midtown Manhattan, east side, *The Panorama of the City of New York*, **2015.**

Digital photograph. © Max Touhey.

Overleaf

Staten Island, Brooklyn, and Queens, *The Panorama of the City of New York*, **2015.**

Digital photograph. © Max Touhey.

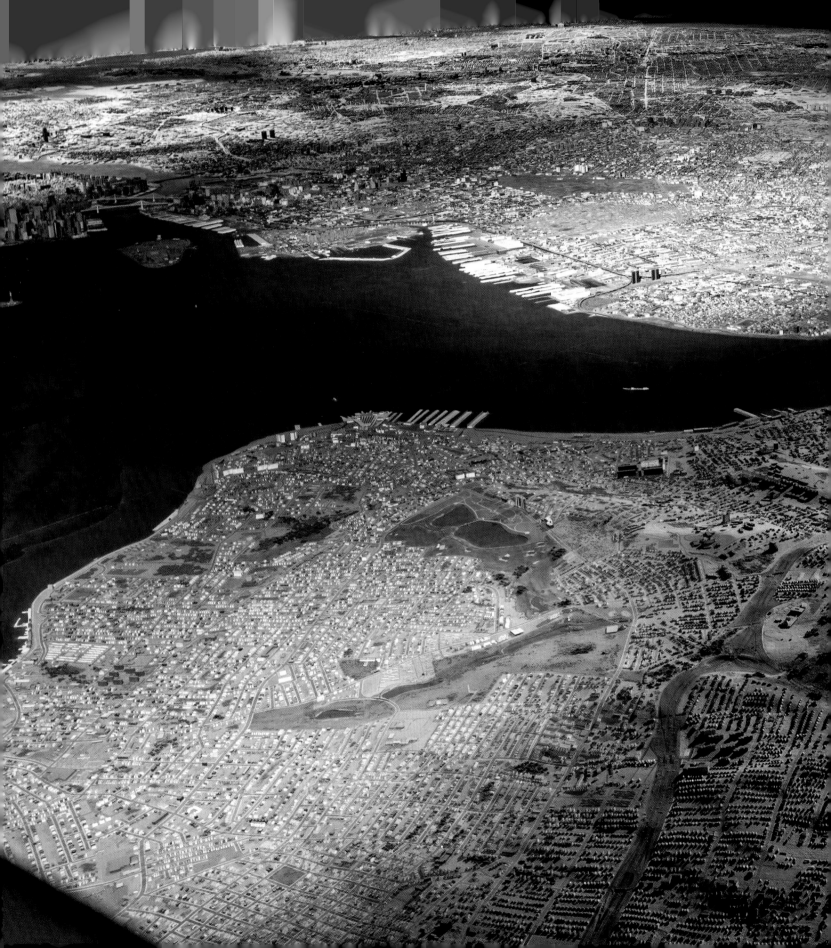

CONTRIBUTOR BIOGRAPHIES

Lauren Haynes is head curator, Governors Island Arts, and vice president for arts and culture at the Trust for Governors Island in New York City. Haynes is a specialist in contemporary art by artists of African descent and has spent her almost two-decade career at art institutions across the US, including the Queens Museum; the Nasher Museum of Art at Duke University; Crystal Bridges Museum of American Art; the Momentary; and the Studio Museum in Harlem. She has written about and lectured extensively on contemporary art and contemporary artists at all stages of their careers.

Haynes serves on the board for the AAMC Foundation as vice president of fundraising and on the visiting committee for the Allen Memorial Art Museum at Oberlin College. Haynes was a 2018 Center for Curatorial Leadership fellow and a recipient of a 2020 ArtTable New Leadership Award. In 2023, President Biden appointed Haynes to the Committee for the Preservation of the White House.

Kenneth T. Jackson is professor emeritus of history at Columbia University, president emeritus of the New-York Historical Society, and editor-in-chief of both editions of *The Encyclopedia of New York City* (1995 and 2010). A popular lecturer, he has been featured on all major television networks and in more than fifty documentary productions. His best-known book is the award-winning *Crabgrass Frontier: The Suburbanization of the United States* (1985).

Lynn Maliszewski is assistant director of archives and collections at the Queens Museum. She cares for and manages objects related to the 1939–1940 and 1964–1965 New York World's Fairs, the art collection, and institutional history. She was previously associate director at Callicoon Fine Arts, New York. She has worked in an archival capacity at Andrea Rosen Gallery, Primary Information, and Printed Matter. Maliszewski is an experienced editor and has written for *BOMB* and *The Brooklyn Rail*, among others, with an emphasis on artists' books and archival projects. She received an MA from the Center for Curatorial Studies, Bard College, in 2017.

Marc H. Miller is a museum consultant, writer, curator, and educator whose work examines the intersections of visual art and popular culture. He is the director of Gallery 98, an online gallery that specializes in art ephemera from the 1960s to '90s. From 1985 to 1991, Miller was a curator at the Queens Museum, where he was responsible for *The Panorama of the City of New York* and the New York World's Fair Collections. His curatorial credits at the Queens Museum include *The Making of the Panorama of the City of New York* (1988); *Remembering the Future: The New York World's Fair from 1939 to 1964* (1989); *Lafayette, Hero of Two Worlds: The Art and Pageantry of His 1824 Farewell Tour of America* (1989); *Louis Armstrong: A Cultural Legacy* (1994); and *Hey! Ho! Let's Go! Ramones and the Birth of Punk* (2016). Miller received a PhD in art history from New York University's Institute of Fine Arts in 1979.

Valerie Paley is senior vice president and the Sue Ann Weinberg Director of the Patricia D. Klingenstein Library at the New-York Historical Society. Formerly the chief historian at the institution, she is founding director of its Center for Women's History, the first such center in the United States within the walls of a major museum. A graduate of Vassar College, Paley holds an MA in American studies and a PhD in history from Columbia University, where she serves on the adjunct faculty at the Columbia Center for American Studies. Her work at New-York Historical encompasses curatorial, scholarly, and administrative responsibilities, including the development of a new joint MA Program in Museum Studies with the CUNY School of Professional Studies, which launched in fall 2019. Paley is the 2020 recipient of the American Historical Association's Herbert Feis Award, which recognizes distinguished contributions to the field of public history.

Vyjayanthi Rao is an anthropologist, writer, and curator, teaching at the Yale School of Architecture. Focusing on memory, heritage, and the built environment, her work explores the intersections of violence, uncertainty, and speculation through scholarly writing and fieldwork in India and the United States. In addition to observant participation through fieldwork, her research draws on sound, image, mapping, and collaborations with visual artists. Rao has published extensively on these subjects; co-curated two major exhibitions for the Lisbon Architecture Triennale (2022) and the Center for Architecture in New York (2023); and participated as an artist in the Kochi Biennale (2016) and the Chicago Biennale of Architecture (2023). She is one of the editors-in-chief of the journal *Public Culture* (Duke University Press).

The Financial District, Manhattan,
The Panorama of the City of New York, **ca. 1963. Installed at New York City Hall in advance of the 1964 opening of the New York World's Fair.**

Scanned medium-format negative. Gift of Lester Associates.

New York
300 years ago
A small trading post
On the tip of Manhattan—

In 1898
Five boroughs
Joined together
To create a city—
Today:
Center of civilization,
This electric metropolis
Has opened opportunity to all,
And its reward
Has been greatness—

Lowell Thomas, "The City of Opportunity" (excerpt)

This edition © Scala Arts Publishers, Inc., 2024

Text © 2024 the authors

First published in 2024 by

Scala Arts Publishers, Inc.
c/o CohnReznick LLP
10th floor, 1301 Avenue of
    the Americas
New York, NY 10019, USA
www.scalapublishers.com
An imprint of B. T. Batsford
    Holdings Ltd.

Queens Museum
New York City Building
Flushing Meadows Corona Park
Queens, NY 11368
www.queensmuseum.org

ISBN 978-1-78551-566-8

Library of Congress Control
Number: 2024945023

Managing Editor: Lynn Maliszewski

Editor: Lauren Haynes

Research: Mayisha Hassan

Text Editor: Erin Barnett

Designer: Rebecca Sylvers,
Miko McGinty Inc.

Printed in China

10 9 8 7 6 5 4 3 2 1

Front cover: The Empire State
Building, *The Panorama of the City
of New York*, 2016. Digital
photograph. © Max Touhey.

Back cover: Workers place
buildings on a section of *The
Panorama of the City of New York*,
ca. 1963. Scanned large-format
negative. Gift of Lester Associates.

Front endpaper: Manhattan, the
Bronx, and Queens, *The Panorama
of the City of New York*, 2015.
Digital photograph. © Max Touhey.

Opposite p. 1: Brooklyn, *The
Panorama of the City of New
York*, 2016. Digital photograph.
© Max Touhey.

Frontispiece: Looking east across
Midtown Manhattan on *The
Panorama of the City of New York*,
ca. 1963. Installed at New York City
Hall in advance of the 1964
opening of the New York World's
Fair. Scanned large-format
negative. Gift of Lester Associates.

pp. 6–7: Central Queens, looking
west toward Manhattan, *The
Panorama of the City of New
York*, 2016. Digital photograph.
© Max Touhey.

Opposite: East side of Manhattan
with Central Park, Roosevelt
Island, and coast of Queens,
*The Panorama of the City of New
York*, 2015. Digital photograph.
© Max Touhey.

Back endpaper: Financial District,
Manhattan, *The Panorama of the
City of New York*, 2015. Digital
photograph. © Max Touhey.

Publication of *The Panorama
of the City of New York* is made
possible by the generosity of
Steven M. Polan as well as
a generous grant from the
Robert David Lion Gardiner
Foundation of New York.

The Queens Museum and
*The Panorama of the City of
New York* are supported by:

National Endowment for the
Arts (NEA)

New York City Department of
Cultural Affairs

New York State Council on
the Arts